# Paddle Your Own Raft

# Paddle Your Own Raft

## OUT OF THE STORM AND INTO THE SUNSHINE

*Marie Elena Hawkins*

Copyright © 2015 by Marie Elena Hawkins

Image of She Never Looked Back used by permission of Shellie Mitchell.

All rights reserved. No part of this book may be reproduced by any mechanical, photographic, or electronic process, nor may it be stored in a retrieval system or otherwise be copied for public or private use—other than for "fair use" as brief quotations embodied in articles and reviews—without prior written permission of the publisher.

The content of this book is not intended as diagnosis or treatment for any physical, mental, or emotional trauma, illness or disease, nor is it intended to be a substitute for care from a licensed medical professional. The intent of the author is to provide general information to individuals seeking to improve their own spiritual and emotional wellbeing. Constitutional rights allow individuals to use this information at their own discretion. The so-called Natural Rules contained within reflect the author's personal views and are open to interpretation. The author and publisher assume no responsibility for any actions taken by the reader.

ISBN: 0692375287
ISBN 13: 9780692375280

*To my precious daughters*
*Natalia & Alexandra*
*my dearest brother Jeff*
*and the memories of*
*my mother Ligia*
*and*
*my Abuela Mencha*

# Table of Contents

1. Introduction · · · · · · · · · · · · · · · · · · · · · · · · · · · 1
2. The Launch · · · · · · · · · · · · · · · · · · · · · · · · · · ·15
3. The Natural Rules · · · · · · · · · · · · · · · · · · · · · · · ·18
4. You and Your Raft · · · · · · · · · · · · · · · · · · · · · · · ·21
5. The Journey · · · · · · · · · · · · · · · · · · · · · · · · · · · 25
6. What is in Your Raft? · · · · · · · · · · · · · · · · · · · 33
7. Who is in Your Raft? · · · · · · · · · · · · · · · · · · · · ·51
8. The Storm of Divorce · · · · · · · · · · · · · · · · · · · · ·77
9. Your Raft, Your Journey · · · · · · · · · · · · · · · · · · · 89
     Acknowledgements · · · · · · · · · · · · · · · · · ·101
     About the Author · · · · · · · · · · · · · · · · · ·105
     About the Artist · · · · · · · · · · · · · · · · · ·105

# Introduction

"This is not how I planned it! How in heaven's name did I get myself into this? Something has to change before I lose my mind."

Any of those sound familiar? Are storms in your life rocking your world in ways you didn't see coming and don't particularly like?

Are you a woman in distress? Do you sometimes wish someone would see your SOS and come rescue you?

You aren't alone. The holistic wellness work I do has gradually expanded into guiding women toward personal empowerment, because it just isn't possible to improve health when life feels out of control.

I created the Paddle Your Own Raft story many years ago as a visualization exercise for my clients so they could step back and see their lives from a totally different perspective.

The story illustrated how we allow circumstances and other people to affect our lives and how we fail to establish or respect healthy boundaries.

As time went on, I discovered that the story could illuminate a wide variety of scenarios, dilemmas, and situations. As I applied it to my own life, it took on deeper meaning and more powerful usefulness.

Paddle Your Own Raft ultimately seeks to modify your frames of reference and open the way for changes that will lead to a deeper, easier satisfaction with your life.

Paddle Your Own Raft is about learning to recognize who and what we carry with us. It's about lightening our loads and letting go of self-imposed stress.

It's also about learning how to go with the flow, and adjust our expectations so that we can enjoy life to the fullest, regardless of the circumstances.

I want to teach you to be discriminating about what you bring into your life, and inspire you to reclaim the dreams you've lost along the way.

Examining personal journeys helps us gain an understanding of how individual actions impact the world we share. I believe we are all energetically and spiritually connected to one another and to all other things in nature, so that whatever energy we emit or send out in thoughts, feelings, and actions affects everything and everyone around us in some way.

Prayer and meditation are important to many women, and you will find many opportunities to include these practices alongside my suggestions.

Before I continue, I want you to know that I use mostly feminine nouns and pronouns throughout this book. It isn't that I don't believe men need to learn to paddle their own rafts; they most definitely do. However, I am speaking to the female psyche and experience more often than not, and I want women to really feel what I am saying.

The standard use of male pronouns to mean men or women subtly alters a woman's reception of the message. If you are a man who is reading this, I welcome you. You will be in the uncommon position of understanding that "she" and "her" may also mean "he" and "him."

There are people in this world who say their lives were dramatically changed for the better by a single momentous event. I am not one of them.

My journey of transformation has involved lots of falling down and getting back up, and more questioning, reading, crying, ranting, praying, and introspection than I can describe.

As my personal situation became increasingly challenging, friends and family members encouraged me to worry less and just go with the flow.

Go with the flow? What flow?! What does that mean exactly? Care to jump into my river and show me how it's done?!

I was tumbling downstream, struggling just to keep my head above water, avoid the rocks, and survive. I was no more capable of going with the flow than sprouting wings and flying away! And trust me, there were many days when flying away was exactly what I wished I could do.

I applied every strategy I knew of, but instead of rising above the chaos, I continued my descent into ever increasing desperation. I was drowning in fear and anxiety, and those emotions took over.

I was good at compartmentalizing and taking care of the tasks at hand, but I was falling apart and incapable of helping myself. No matter how hard I tried, I was quickly losing touch with the kinder, more understanding woman I was trying to be.

Over fifteen years of crises and complications in my life, followed by two crushing and unexpected losses, finally overwhelmed me. I commented to a friend that I could no longer hold back the ocean. And one day, I just gave up.

I curled up that night feeling such utter desolation, there was simply no fight left in me. And for the first time in over a year, I fell into a blessedly sound sleep.

The next morning I woke up feeling like the weight of the world had been lifted from my shoulders. It was as though the ocean I had spent years trying to hold back had just receded on its own. It was still out there, just as my deep sorrow for what I had lost was still with me, but the dark clouds of fearfulness and anxiety had finally lifted.

It was like standing on a beach just before dawn. The sun hadn't come up yet, but there was a calm sky, and the promise of a brighter new day ahead.

Over the next few months, it became clearer to me how I had made my life much more difficult and stressful by fighting the current at every turn.

I had been fearfully obsessed with the unknown future. Every difficulty was a crisis that I had to solve. Failure was not an option I was willing to accept. I couldn't simply experience each moment as it unfolded, and that was the crux of my problem.

Going with the flow meant just being present without trying to fix anything. It didn't mean I had to be okay with the situation. It just meant that resisting it wasn't the answer. I hadn't yet grasped that surrender and acceptance does not equal failure.

Oh, the beauty of hindsight. If only I'd known. I fervently wish I had learned those lessons much earlier in my life, but apparently my soul has required the "school of hard knocks" method of learning, with plenty of hands-on experiences.

After taking a bumpy, convoluted route to wisdom's door, I finally acknowledged in the depths of my heart and soul that life really wasn't meant to be such an ordeal. My own great and small choices and agreements had made it so.

The "life is hard and not fair" paradigm is powerful, and in accepting it as inevitable truth we subconsciously create endless scenarios in which we constantly struggle to get where we think we want to go. We miss amazing opportunities, as well as the silver linings in many of our dark clouds.

The path toward holistic (whole person) wellness requires a deeper understanding of who we are, how we got where we are, and what we want in our lives.

Knowing what kind of life we truly wish to have makes it a lot easier to create, but most of us don't have a clear vision of the whole picture.

We neglect to take care of the small details that add up to our lives, stumbling through our busy days with the awareness that something is missing, but not knowing what to do about it. The opposite problem is fixating on insignificant details and missing the larger picture.

Either way, we feel dissatisfied with our lives and miss out on many opportunities to be happier.

One of the greatest driving forces behind basic human behavior is love. We need to be accepted, loved, wanted, and appreciated, and we will do almost anything to achieve these needs.

We are molded by our families, our societies, and our need to belong. We may suppress our aspirations or opinions to fit in or to keep the peace.

We may stifle our needs and our wants to avoid conflict and because we have been taught to put others first. The result can be a lifelong denial of the deepest needs and desires of our essential self.

The saddest part of silencing our soul's inner voice is that we become disconnected from who we are, what we like, and how we want to live.

While in the middle of a workshop a few years ago, a client suddenly exclaimed, "don't ask me these open ended questions! I don't know what I like or what I want anymore!"

Some women fabricate an entire life according to someone else's ideals, but at some point the façade will begin to crack.

First, your inner voice will try to get your attention, and then your body will start kicking it up a few notches at a time. Holistic practitioners know that hidden stress is behind a vast number of health issues.

A degree of conformity is a necessary part of creating a place for ourselves within our societies and families. The key is to stay true to our essential nature and purpose—simple to say but not so easy to achieve.

Putting ourselves first doesn't imply being selfish in the traditional sense. Healthy, beneficial selfishness does not conflict with kindness, consideration, or integrity.

Putting yourself first means respecting the deepest needs of your essential self. Developing your highest potential and sharing your gifts can only benefit everyone around you.

The greatest philosophers and spiritual leaders agree that every worthwhile purpose is equal in importance. The purpose doesn't have to be extraordinarily grand; it just needs to be genuine.

Our roles, jobs, and responsibilities transform over time, just as our purpose during different phases of life changes.

A worthwhile purpose normally involves using one's special gifts and talents to their highest potential for good. But some purposes may not always appear to be positive ones at the outset.

I suspect that some difficult people show up in our lives to help us develop patience and character, or to steer us toward the paths we're supposed to be on.

Consider the irresponsible taxi driver who picks you up late and causes you to miss your flight. Then that plane crashes. Was it his purpose to save your life? He surely didn't plan it that way, but he played a pretty important role in your life that day.

It took some time for the dust to settle after my personal chapter of disaster, but I clearly remember the morning I finally sat down to take stock of where I was financially, and said out loud to myself, "Ok. Well. I guess I'm not supposed to coast anytime soon." Thank you… I think.

We all face an assortment of storms; ups and downs, losses, and life changing events. But even minor things can add up, while major life stressors are often beyond our control. At some point, we begin to stumble.

It isn't easy to move forward when we are weighed down with fatigue, anxiety and uncertainty. We lose the ability to think clearly, respond appropriately, or recognize possible solutions. I see increasing numbers of women who are desperately at the end of their ropes. I've been there, and it isn't a good place to be.

Keep in mind that stress is not a thing, an event, or a disease. It is just one of many possible responses to everything and everyone we experience in our lives. These response triggers are called stressors.

It's important to note that not all stressors are negative in nature. Weddings, new jobs, and new babies are usually very happy events, for example, but they do require significant adjustments and can create unexpected and unpredictable stress.

Positive or negative, when stressors occur simultaneously or one right after the other, as they often seem to do, life easily becomes overwhelming. Add financial uncertainty to the mix, and things can become immeasurably more complicated.

The lack of financial security alone is arguably one of the most serious stressors of our time. It's true that money isn't everything, but the lack of it can transform any situation into a much more stressful one.

Increasing tax burdens hinder our ability to get ahead, retirement funds are dwindling in value, and job security may be a thing of the past.

Poor health, runaway health insurance costs and out of pocket medical expenses literally add insult to injury. Staggering medical bills are the number one cause of bankruptcy in our country today.

Even without extraordinary complications, any stressor can be significantly intensified by financial concerns.

Family members scattered across the country lack the resources to visit as often as they'd like, and each generation loses out on family support systems that have held societies together throughout history.

Desperately needed rest and vacations are common casualties of tightened budgets.

People work at jobs they despise just for the paycheck. I see this much too often, and most people don't realize that lack of job satisfaction is one of the strongest predictors of poor health and premature death across all economic levels.

We "do it ourselves" to save money, even when this means further physical and mental exhaustion. We may be unable to do all our yard work or pay to have it done, but neither can we downsize, because selling our current home at an acceptable price is close to impossible.

Many women find themselves still raising children while dealing with their own or their spouse's wellness issues, as well as their parents' declining health.

This "sandwich" situation is especially prevalent today because so many of us had our children later in life than was common a generation or two ago.

College graduates all over the country are unemployed or underemployed–unable to keep up with student loan debt, much less make progress toward becoming financially independent.

According to the 2012 U. S. Census, well over a third of young adults under the age of 32 live with their parents; the highest rates in at least forty years.

Adult children with their own kids live with parents, who themselves are trying to care for their own aging parents. Or, the aging parents find themselves with little choice but to move in with adult children.

Over half of today's grandparents are either raising their grandchildren or providing full time child care and financial support, as parents work multiple jobs or go back to school to fulfill personal or financial goals.

Women who thought their child rearing years were over, and who had just begun to pursue their own interests and leisure activities, suddenly find their lives turned upside down in order to practically raise a family for the second time.

The toll of all this on mental and physical health, as well as on marriages and relationships is significant.

Baby boomers between ages 50 and 69 currently make up the highest divorce rate age group in the country. This "gray divorce" trend is leaving thousands of us facing precarious financial futures at a time when we are least able to make up for the losses.

While women initiate most "gray" divorces, many more remain in miserable marriages because they fear becoming homeless if they leave.

Approximately 55% of women over 65 now live alone; some are widows, many are divorced, and a few never married. Aging when living alone presents its own unique concerns and challenges, although the perks of living alone are not to be underestimated, either.

All of these multi-generational situations require us to redefine our roles and make countless major and minor adjustments.

It isn't my intention to focus on gloom and doom. I only want to acknowledge that for many of us right now, life is far from simple or easy. It's quite likely that several of the women around you are in at least one of these situations. I am, and perhaps you are too.

These endless demands on dwindling emotional, mental, physical, and monetary resources can leave us feeling exhausted, depressed, cranky, and totally "stressed out."

There was a time when stressors were acute, short-term events. You ran for your life and either outran your pursuer or met your demise. Hunger was a common longer term worry, but again, had a clear-cut ending; you obtained food or you died. Today, things are different in that we face many "no end in sight" situations, causing what is called chronic stress.

The vast majority of modern day stressors are not going anywhere anytime soon. We can, however, diminish the power they have over us, and learn to let go of self-imposed stress. Perhaps one of the most critical aspects to today's stressors is the sense of having lost all control over what happens to us.

Control is a multi-faceted concept that's hard to define. Psychology teaches us about locus of control.

An internal locus of control is the conviction that we have control over our lives; we can adjust our behavior to achieve the results we wish to see.

An external locus of control is the belief that we are at the mercy of fate, God, circumstances, other people, or genes.

I have a fairly strong internal locus of control, yet on countless occasions throughout my life, I failed to act on my own behalf.

I allowed all sorts of external factors to dictate where I went and how I would get there, blaming my troubles on external circumstances and situations beyond my control.

I didn't go looking for problems. I was smart and strong and capable, and determined to make things work out right, come hell or high water.

Care to guess how that attitude worked out for me?

The events I refer to as storms are a normal part of life and when they last a few hours or days, they are fairly manageable. The storms that last for months or years eventually overwhelm our ability to cope effectively.

Life really is a kind of journey and learning to make the most of it is a lifelong process. It has taken me a long time to truly understand how I got here.

Over the years, I have read the works of dozens of teachers, spiritual leaders, and philosophers, including *The Four Agreements* by Don Miguel Ruiz, *This Thing*

*Called You* by Ernest Holmes, and a number of books by Marianne Williamson, Paulo Coelho, and others.

I am forever grateful for their insights and influence in helping prepare me for deeper truths, and offering me the revelations and guidance I needed when I was ready for it. I wasn't always able to "get into" some books the first go around.

The reality is that we can only take in and use what we are emotionally and spiritually ready to receive. If you are still reading this, it means you are ready to take a few steps forward with me, and I am honored.

My goal with the simple little story that follows is twofold; to help you visualize your journey in a way that prepares you for greater understanding, and to give you some valuable tools for creating meaningful change in your life.

You can paddle through the storm that is getting you down and into the sunshine of a brighter tomorrow.

I want to rock your world with a paradigm shift that changes everything for you starting today!

# The Launch

Before we begin, the raft we are going to picture in our minds is something resembling a wooden rowboat or an inflatable rubber raft; one with rope hand holds, a seat, and a sturdy but slightly flexible shape. It is sized for a single person.

Read the short story below once or twice, then close your eyes and picture the scene. Make it vividly realistic and richly filled with images of anything that pleases you. Let the imagery unfold for a few minutes before you continue reading.

*It's a perfect day. You are standing alone on the bank of a beautiful stream. Everything around you makes you feel happy to be alive. The moving water gurgles as it flows, and you hear an occasional splash as the current stumbles over rocks in its path. There is a small raft on the bank and you know it is yours. You are compelled to get in it and take up the paddle. Before you know it, you are heading downstream.*

So there you are, happily paddling along when you see a beautiful place further ahead. It looks inviting and interesting. You really want to paddle over there. Maybe you want to rest or even explore a bit. But no matter how hard you paddle, you just can't seem to make any progress at all.

You turn around and are startled to discover your spouse, partner, children, in-laws, parents, boss, or maybe even your grandchildren or siblings in your raft with you. And they all have their own paddles. And they are all paddling your raft in the direction they each want to go!

I can see you smiling, nodding your head and maybe even laughing right now, because you know exactly what I'm talking about.

But it isn't really funny, is it?

It no longer surprises me to see women in tears when the full impact of this image hits them.

This is your raft, your life.

When and how did you lose control of it?

When your raft is weighed down with other people, no one is getting where they want to go, least of all you.

Most importantly, if you don't do something, your raft will eventually be swamped.

Many of us don't even try to lighten our loads until the water reaches our chins, or we realize we are going to drown if we don't do something.

## Paddle Your Own Raft

It's no wonder we suddenly find ourselves wishing we could abandon ship or angrily shouting at everyone to abandon ours, but really it is our own soul's attention we are trying to get.

If you regularly feel restless, listless, trapped, frustrated, unhappy or dissatisfied with your life, it's time to re-examine your position, alter your course, and make some significant changes. Easier said than done? Absolutely.

It is well accepted that we are only willing to make a change when we reach the point at which the pain of staying where we are is worse than the pain of moving forward.

Will your changing "rock the boat?" Absolutely! Any major adjustments you make will likely rock your raft and everyone else's around you.

Putting people back into their own rafts will not be easy for you or them. The fact remains, however, that everyone needs to be paddling their own rafts.

You must understand one very crucial aspect of discovering loads of people in your raft. You let them get in. You gave each and every one of them permission, and in some cases, you actually sent them irresistible invitations!

You might have handed over your paddle, or you might even have become a powerless passenger in your own raft.[*]

---

[*] Note: Crime victims, children, and mentally impaired persons have no responsibility for offenders who forcibly invade their "rafts". If you have been the victim of any type of crime or abuse, I encourage you to seek professional help to remove any form of offender from your raft.

# The Natural Rules

*Every person gets his or her own raft and paddle. You don't get to choose your raft.*

*No raft is better than another, and no two rafts are exactly alike.*

*You only get one raft for this journey. Each raft is perfectly designed for its owner and her journey.*

*It is up to you to take care of your raft. You, and you alone, are responsible for it.*

*It doesn't matter where you launch from. Everyone starts at a different place.*

*We all occupy the same body of water; always connected to, and affected by, one another.*

*You will never be totally alone on your journey, although you may sometimes think you are.*

*Most legs of your journey will be in the company of others; who and how is often up to you.*

*There will be those who believe theirs is the only way, but in fact, each soul must find its own path.*

*The journey is neither a race nor a competition.*

*You always move downstream. No amount of paddling can ever propel you upstream or back to where you started.*

*Very little of what lies ahead or beneath is visible at any given time.*

*The view, seasons, weather, and surroundings will endlessly and sometimes unexpectedly change.*

*Day always follows night. The sunshine always returns after the worst storms.*

*You will encounter obstacles, whirlpools, waterfalls, rapids, storms, still waters, and more.*

*There is no way of knowing where the stream may lead, how many times it might curve or branch off, or when it will become part of a river.*

*There will be many stops along the way. Some will be more pleasant than others.*

*Expectations about the journey tend to result in correlating experiences.*

*You will be presented with an infinite number of choices to make along the way.*

*Every choice–great or small–results in intended and unintended consequences.*

*Everything you experience is a consequence of the choices that you and others have made.*

*Learning from wise and poor choices or experiences makes for a smoother journey.*

*Guidance comes from within and without, and you may or may not choose to heed it.*

*Opportunities for learning are regularly presented and often repeated as necessary.*

*There is no telling how long the journey will be or how quickly or easily the destination will be reached.*

*The journey is more important than the destination.*

*How one handles each leg of the journey shapes the perceived success at its end, and may determine the final destination.*

*Everyone eventually reaches the final destination.*

# You and Your Raft

LET'S IMAGINE THAT THE PERSON paddling the raft is the essential you–the genuine soul and energy of your being. This essence that is you has intellectual, spiritual, and emotional feelings, needs, personality, dreams, and valuable gifts—your essential nature.

The essential you is what remains when the physical trappings (body, name, labels, etc.) of earthly life are removed.

The essential you is perfectly human, which means that whatever you consider to be imperfections are actually in keeping with the state of being human. It's time to redefine your image of "perfect". The essential you is raw perfection. It is learned perception, attitude and behavior that need adjusting.

When your intellectual/spiritual/emotional states are in alignment with your soul's purpose and your body's physical abilities, the result is a satisfying and amazingly powerful state of harmony that makes all things possible.

In other words, when *who you are* is in sync with *how you are living*, you achieve satisfying contentment and the ability to do virtually anything you desire.

We've all experienced isolated moments of this harmony. The goal is to experience it more often.

Your raft represents your physical body and the space you occupy in place and time. All the journey's experiences, feelings, memories, dreams, hopes, joys, pains, and so forth, are stored in your raft and become a part of you. Think of your raft as being your soul's means of transportation for this journey we call life.

Each and every raft serves an essential purpose: to get its occupant down the river to its destination. Therefore, the very existence of a raft gives it intrinsic value equal to that of every other raft in existence.

Each human body is created with a unique set of physical characteristics and genetic potentials. Genes and epigenetics determine body type, race, eye color, skin color, gender, sexual orientation, left or right hand dominance, hair color and type, height potential, and more. Just like the raft and its paddler, you and your body are one for this journey.

There is no "standard model" human or raft. Every single one is different from the rest. Some will have apparent factory defects, and others will appear to have luxury option packages. Every raft is specifically designed for its owner and his or her personal journey.

Some are built for speed; others for slow cruising. Some are quite durable; others tend to fall apart easily.

Some are designed for getting out into the middle; others are shore huggers. Plain or fancy, brown, white, red, yellow, black or multicolored, elegant or shabby, striped or flowery, graceful or awkward, quiet or creaky, broad and sturdy or small and light—the river is filled with a mindboggling assortment of rafts.

You can decorate and remodel yours all you want—sand, seal, paint, coat it in glitter, or reconstruct it—but the raft you get is the raft you ride to the end.

Let's take a moment to consider a real raft. Can you picture a well-kept raft? The sides are sturdy but somewhat flexible. The bottom is watertight and strong. The finishes are all in great shape, protecting the integrity of the craft.

If you maintain it well, it will see you through many different situations and miles of travel, easily carrying you through calm and rough water, taking you anywhere you wish to go.

Imagine this same raft after years of neglect; battered by storms and scraped against countless rocks and unseen debris. It may start springing leaks, requiring great effort to steer and bailing to stay afloat. The paddler finds herself limiting the distances and places this raft can go. Trying to patch and fix things once they are badly deteriorated is really difficult.

But it's not enough to take care of only the exterior. The integrity and strength of your raft is determined by everything that impacts your emotions, your health, your mind, and your ability to function. Therefore, whatever you bring into your raft is of great importance with significant consequences.

Negative, harmful baggage can eat away at the raft from the inside out, and is just as dangerous to the integrity of your raft as any physical damage.

Of course, over time, every raft (each body) will deteriorate to some degree. No matter what we do, age, wear, and life's mileage take their toll, and sooner or later, the raft will cease to be.

The goal is to not let this happen prematurely. The intention is to maximize age and mileage, while minimizing wear and tear.

# The Journey

Picture yourself enjoying the experience with no particular expectation or destination in mind. Imagine calm water, blue skies, perfect weather—a stretch of water where you could just put down your paddle and drift with the current. Oh yes, sparkling, quiet, gentle, drifting…

Well, I don't know about you, but after a little while, I'd be bored out of my mind!

I need generous amounts of quiet alone time, but like most people, I am physically, emotionally, and spiritually energized by actively using my body and brain on a regular basis.

We aren't supposed to drift aimlessly for our entire lives, yet most of us fail to grasp the power of taking time between bursts of activity to stop paddling, be still, appreciate the scenery, and see where the current might take us—that we might use our abilities to enjoy our lives in unexpected ways.

We are born with great potential and special talents. Some of these are recognized and developed when we are young, but many more are the result of a lifetime of simply living our lives.

Most women greatly underestimate how many skills they have acquired. A huge stumbling block I see with my clients is the assumption that if they couldn't do it when they were younger, they can't do it now. ("it" could be anything)

There are countless famous "late bloomers" who didn't make their marks until later in life. Laura Ingalls Wilder wrote her first Little House book when she was 64. Artist Grandma Moses began to paint at age 79. Actress Betty White is at the peak of her popularity in her nineties. It's never too late to start a new chapter.

Have you ever considered that you may be drawn to something for a reason? I have no doubt that we like things related to whatever would truly satisfy the purpose we were born to fulfill. If you've always imagined yourself doing, learning, or making something specific, it just might be because you have special talents or gifts that would really shine if used appropriately within that longed-for realm.

This doesn't necessarily mean that if you love music, for example, you are to become a talented or famous musician. It might be that you would enjoy owning a music store, writing for a music industry publication, or studying the benefits of music on the brain.

Whatever you focus on is what you draw to you. This may be associated with the law of attraction these days, but it isn't a new age concept. Most ancient spiritual and religious philosophies contain some version of "as within, so without."

*"I am learning that if you focus on what you want, (peace) instead of what you don't want, (war) you will receive it in abundance!"* Mother Teresa

I will never forget the advice of a classmate's father, a professional driver, who once drove us to a school event across the state when we were teens just learning to drive. If we ever found ourselves faced with an unexpected obstacle or vehicle in our path, he explained, we should never focus on it. Instead, we must always find and aim for the "hole"—the escape route with the best chance for survival.

Having a specific goal or purpose in mind helps you make the many corrections in course that keep you moving in the right direction.

I am certain that if you are destined to fulfill that goal or purpose, whatever is necessary for your success will be placed in your path. Whether or not you choose to accept those gifts is another issue entirely.

Of course, sometimes we may have allowed ourselves to be blown so far off course, it takes a major storm to put us back on the path we were supposed to follow.

The tsunami that hit my life a few years ago was the most difficult period I've ever gone through, and it has totally changed the direction of my journey.

People I loved and my responsibilities to them were swept away. I still don't understand why it had to happen the way it did, but maybe I was meant to go where they were not meant to follow, or perhaps their purposes in life had been fulfilled.

Whatever purpose I am destined to fulfill is not yet clear to me, but there is no doubt in my mind that my tsunami came about to help get me there.

I was forced to examine my "self" and deal with my baggage. I was given the opportunity to change, make some repairs, put a fresh coat of paint on my raft, and begin a totally new leg of my journey.

I don't believe in coincidences, but I do believe in a purposeful universe. I have been amazed at the special people who almost magically arrived at my side at the exact moment I needed them, doors to opportunities that opened without my knocking on them, or the book that kept "randomly" appearing in my life when I most needed its message.

I have developed absolute confidence in the notion that as long as I move in the right direction, life will support and reward my efforts in every possible way. If I get off track, the obstacles will reappear.

I have faith that my journey is supposed to be a good one. If I can be true to myself, prioritize the integrity of my raft, and paddle in accordance with my purposes as they change, my life can be more than good; it can be grand!

*Paddle Your Own Raft*

It is not our place to decide how another person's journey should be made. We should realize that while we are all on the same river, none of us are on the same journey. Some journeys will be easier, and some will be more complicated. We can offer assistance and advice, but ultimately we must accept that we each have our own rafts and our own journeys, and we can't paddle another person's raft or make their journey for them.

Each of us may or may not seek guidance and direction on our journeys, and we may make terrible decisions, but those choices and their corresponding consequences are ours to make and answer to.

Establishing healthy boundaries will be one of the most crucial steps you take in creating a life that brings you the maximum amount of joy and satisfaction, and the minimum amount of pain and turmoil. We each have our own unique personal healthy boundary line.

In our raft scenario, the personal space around your raft, where your life meets the rest of the world, is an imaginary, but almost tangible, boundary line.

Your personal healthy boundary line is the edge of your comfort zone—where contact and intimacy are welcome or unwelcome, and where acceptable and unacceptable behavior meet. It is where you decide what you will, or will not allow or tolerate in your life.

Moment-to-moment circumstances, your cultural upbringing, and your individual personality and mood, will determine the magnitude of your personal space.

In the most intimate moments, such as mothers with their infants, or lovers with their beloved, these boundaries temporarily disappear, as we allow another's raft to meld with ours to varying degrees.

In summary, each journey is personalized and cannot be compared to anyone else's.

The journey is neither a race nor a competition. Some will be made in a short time, while others take a century. Each one will do it differently. It's not up to us to judge the worth of anyone else's journey.

As far as I know, only one thing is certain; we all eventually reach the end of our individual journeys and arrive at the final destination.

There will be no prizes for arrival time, for having the flashiest raft, the most expensive finish, or for being the most popular raft on the river. Some rafts will arrive looking barely used, while others will come in looking so battered and worn out, it's amazing they made it so far.

In any case, regardless of its condition, upon reaching the final destination, the raft will fade away. Having served its purpose, it is no longer needed. It was only ever meant to carry us this far.

All of us have different beliefs about what happens at the final destination. Heaven, hell, purgatory, reincarnation, nothingness—these are but a few of the things that people believe might follow death.

I personally don't think there is a single right answer. Just as we each have unique journeys on this earth, I believe we probably experience different versions of various destinations when we die. But, the truth is, it doesn't matter what I think. Each of us will find out when our time comes.

However, I am fairly sure that how one makes the journey shapes its perceived success in the end, and may also help determine the final destination.

# What is in Your Raft?

## Experience

I believe that one of the primary issues impacting our current stress levels is the lack of appropriate models for many of the situations we are dealing with.

Although many of us are facing similar worries and problems, the circumstances surrounding them are unlike anything we have experienced or witnessed before.

Throughout history, major events like the industrial revolution or pandemic plague have caused tumultuous upheavals as people adjusted to a changed world.

We are in the midst of social and technological changes that are occurring at lightning speed.

No wonder we feel lost and anxious. We don't know how to manage or respond to many of these events and we are more weighed down than ever before by baggage and stressors.

We are trying to find our way through unfamiliar territory and we are attempting to create new models of behavior, action, and response—all at the same time.

Remember my mention of a paradigm shift in the introduction?

A paradigm [pare-a-dime] is a concept based on a specific set of beliefs and assumptions. What we believe to be true is based on a given paradigm.

For example, the earth being the center of the universe was such a long-held paradigm that persons who challenged it sometimes risked their lives to do so. Changing this paradigm took centuries, and it altered science, religion, and society in ways that were mind-boggling at the time.

**A paradigm shift is not just a change of heart or acceptance of a new concept; it is the discarding of the old concept as being erroneous and no longer pertinent to the future, while allowing a totally different concept to take its place.**

I want you to leave behind the paradigm that life is supposed to be hard and not fair, and replace it with the paradigm that life is good. Life presents us with endless opportunities for positive growth and joy.

No, I'm not delusional. Believing life is good doesn't mean I expect only pleasant things. Accepting the "life is good" paradigm requires the acquisition of faith in a better future, and the letting go of groundless fears.

It's not that life isn't fair, it's that we fail to heed our inner guidance systems. We don't listen to that little voice that tries to warn us. We pretend not to see the red flags. We ignore the tightness in our bellies and the thumping of our hearts.

Life continually tries to get us back on track, but we insist on making the process more painful and chaotic than it was meant to be.

I've already told you about the time in my life that stressed me out so badly I lost the ability to think or act clearly. I allowed paralyzing fear to rule my life.

There was no end in sight and I fully expected things to get much worse. I was so bogged down in anxiety, imagining the awfulness that was sure to come, that I was scarcely able to live in the present.

My situation came to a swift and difficult end when I least expected it, but none of the things I had feared and worried about happened. What actually transpired were events I never considered possible.

All those years of over the top stress and misery—for nothing. And worse, it caused me to miss out on many moments of joy that might have been.

Most storms have many good things to offer us. The loss of needless fear was one of the more valuable lessons of my mega storm. This book was one of the gifts. Silver linings I never imagined.

I have no doubt that painful events and situations are part of life, and I'm sure I'll encounter others in the years to come. I just have confidence that the good days will far outnumber the bad, and that I will be better at responding to it all than I was in the past.

Be aware of your thoughts and words. It is good to vent and let pain or fear out from time to time, but obsessing about it only strengthens its presence in your raft. At some point, you must choose to release it or be forever encumbered by it.

What about the pain of losing a loved one? How can death possibly be part of the "life is good" paradigm? All I can say is that death is the natural and inevitable end to every journey, be it short or long.

Some deaths are easier to bear than others. The death of my elderly grandmother at 105 saddened me, but the totally unexpected death of my very young looking mother at 81 was a stunning blow.

The circumstances surrounding the death can make a difference, as can the state of our relationship with the person at the time of their death. Premature deaths are particularly hard, especially when these are the result of accidents, suicide, or foul play.

The loss of a child is most certainly a devastating experience I pray I never have.

Each individual must find his or her own way of moving forward following the death of a loved one. I will not attempt to address our society's religious and non-religious perspectives on death and dying. I have my own, and while they bring me a degree of peace, I still cry and hurt and miss my loved ones every day.

My beliefs, however, help me pick my paddle back up and get on with the business of living the days remaining to me to the best of my ability. I believe our loved ones would not wish us to suffer endlessly and remain stuck in a state of grief.

Many terrible things have no apparent rhyme or reason, and this too, is part of life—a friend dies in an auto accident, a tornado levels a whole town. These things happen, and we may never understand why.

Every word, every action, and every event, no matter how tragic, how grand or how insignificant, results in mind-boggling effects, most of which we will never be aware.

Science is discovering that our very thoughts and intentions affect the quantum fabric of time and space in ways we can barely comprehend. We have the capacity to effect incredible changes, but we lack the conviction and ability to do it very well.

I grew up beside a lake and learned that waves often reached the shore long after the boat that created them had passed from sight. So too, my actions create ripples, swells, and choppy waves far beyond my ability to see them.

*Every choice—great or small—results in intended and unintended consequences.*

After an ugly argument over undone laundry, someone storms out, drives away, and causes a terrible accident in which several people die. The lives of countless people have now been forever changed—for better, for worse, or both.

Estranged family members come together to grieve and end up re-establishing loving contact. A position opens up for someone who had no job the day before, while insurance money makes college possible for still another.

The ripple effect of a single silly argument on the surface of our shared river rocked the rafts of some, and smoothed the water for others.

Unintended consequences roll on.

Then, there are the many opportunities for spreading purely good experiences—the encouraging word, a smile, a moment of assistance—all those things we offer without the expectation of anything in return. The "pay it forward" movement highlights the positive ongoing effects of random acts of kindness. Heightening your awareness of the opportunities for spreading kindness increases your ability to do so.

Don't be surprised if unusual things happen when you make these gestures. One Christmas, I felt strongly compelled to tip the elderly gentleman bagging my groceries. I knew I had a five-dollar bill in my pocket because it was the last money I had. Imagine my shock when the bill that emerged from my pocket was a twenty. I never figured out how it got there or what happened to my five but he must have needed $20. I'm still in awe, although I've had other similarly remarkable experiences.

Love, laughter, kindness, and other good things are radiant, weightless energy that bring joy and satisfaction to our lives. You have the power to choose to fill your raft with these wonderful things and spread their beautiful effects like ripples on the water.

A man once chased me down in a bustling foreign airport to return a favorite scarf that I had unknowingly dropped. He was happy to have caught up with me; I was grateful to not have lost my scarf. It was nothing earth shattering, but I am reminded of his kindness every time I wear it, and it still makes me feel good inside. It naturally inspires me to pass it on.

Experiences begin to shape us from the moment we take our first breaths. Even events that take place before we are born have been shown to affect us.

Children born to stressed mothers tend to be fussier and more sensitive to stressors themselves. Emotionally neglected infants have difficulty establishing emotional ties and relating to others for the rest of their lives. Infants whose mothers play music during their pregnancies demonstrate response to the same pieces after they're born.

Your personal collection of family, community, and cultural experiences shapes the person you become—everything you sense, feel, see, taste, hear, smell, learn, create, or imagine. The process doesn't stop until you take your last breath.

Positive, feel good experiences make us feel happy and loved, and drive us to seek more of the same. If we are fortunate, our rafts are filled with memorable experiences that fill us with contentment and satisfaction.

Some experiences are neutral and innocuous, like discovering that eating sand isn't particularly pleasant.

Events like touching a hot iron result in our avoidance of things that could seriously harm us. Unpleasant events we observe or experience in our family or community shape our thinking and behavior. We don't usually carry these types of experiences with us in terribly negative ways; they just help us learn about the world we live in.

Generally speaking, the more varied and richer our personal pool of experiences is, the better we're able to adapt to changes in our lives.

## Baggage

Emotionally painful experiences, however, often become excess baggage.

Are you carrying excess baggage in your raft? I can see you nodding emphatically as you say, "boy, am I ever!" You might have even said that out loud. I probably should have asked you how *much* baggage you are carrying.

Every scary or hurtful word, look, or event has the potential to become excess baggage that we carry with us all our lives.

We all accumulate a variety of bundles of junky baggage in our rafts. Most of us have virtual piles of baggage that are so jumbled, we no longer know what all we carry around, where it all came from, why we still have it, or why we can't throw it out.

What about intensely painful emotional baggage? I want you to imagine it as dense, heavy, negative energy. It creates very real perceptions of weight, and our language reflects this. We speak of the "loads we bear", or feeling "weighed down" by sorrow, and so forth.

Epigenetic science can now monitor and measure changes in the body's energy fields and genetic makeup, and this allows us to see how our emotions and thoughts can create biologically measurable changes in the body and to the genes themselves.

When we obsessively think about people or events that have caused us distress, we must realize that these intangible thoughts create negative effects that harm us emotionally and biologically.

There were years in which life kept dropping what I referred to as "monkey wrenches" on me. With the encouragement of a wise friend, I reimagined them as stars carrying hidden blessings—although I did say the points were painfully sharp.

Immediately re-framing a difficult event as a gift in disguise is much easier than transforming a piece of time hardened baggage into a positive experience.

Baggage that carries deep negative emotions and thoughts is truly damaging. The goal is to let go of as much as possible, and avoid adding more to your load. There is plenty of ugliness and anger in the world, and keeping it out of your raft isn't always easy.

I like the image of my raft within a strong beautiful bubble that only allows good energy to pass through; anything negative or harmful simply bounces right off. Knowing that this magic bubble can be created anywhere and anytime is powerful stuff, and many of my clients have used this image successfully anytime they encounter someone or something unpleasant.

The images and energy patterns of severe trauma or abuse are extremely heavy baggage that are especially difficult to get rid of.

Energy based psychology offers an entirely new way of treating victims, and has been used with great success in areas devastated by war and sexual assault. The results for all types of post-traumatic stress are said to be nothing short of amazing.

The premise is that trauma saturates a person's natural energy field with harmful negative energy frequencies. The person may feel stuck and unable to let go of their pain. No amount of conventional therapy seems to help for very long.

Energy based techniques, however, involve replacing the harmful negative energy field with positive, healing energy, allowing the person to finally feel relieved of their burden.

This modality does not bring up or seek to erase memories; it just allows the person to move past the trauma so that healing can finally begin.

Energy psychology is still in its infancy and practitioners are not easy to find. I am hopeful that as knowledge of its effectiveness spreads, so will its use.

Energy healing modalities should not be reserved just for those suffering the effects of severe trauma. Anyone who is stuck in a cycle of emotional pain or depression can benefit, and I know that it works.

Following a complicated year of mourning, I found myself struggling with overwhelming grief for the first time in my life. Then, while on a trip, I received an incredible energy based "shamanic" healing session.

I wasn't looking for this type of healing, but I somehow ended up exactly where I needed to be in order to cross paths with this special woman when I most needed what only she could offer. I know in the depths of my soul that this was no coincidence, and any skepticism I might have had about this ancient practice was totally erased by my experience.

The movement of my own energy waves through my body was startling, but that was only a small part of the total effect. By the next day I felt as though the heavy veil of sorrow that had shrouded me was removed. The sadness was still there, but it no longer smothered me in gloom. I can honestly say that a dramatic new level of healing began for me that day.

## Stowaways

The invisible persons hiding in your raft are stowaways. Created by strong negative emotions, *guilt stowaways, ghost voice stowaways, and perpetrator stowaways are* especially tenacious and hard to remove from our rafts.

There are countless strategies for ridding our rafts of stowaways, but many will be beyond the scope of this book. If my tips are not enough to address your situation, and you are being seriously affected by it, please don't hesitate to seek professional help.

**Guilt voice stowaways** are created by what you may have done to or failed to do for another person.

Guilt voices are extraordinarily heavy baggage, and can drain the life force from you as effectively as any disease.

It doesn't matter whether you are truly guilty of wrongdoing, your own guilt voice can be deafening and relentless. Forgiving oneself is even harder than forgiving another person, but punishing yourself over and over again will not erase what happened.

Do your best to make amends for any wrongs you have done. Ask and accept forgiveness from God, the universe, or the person you wronged, even if that person is no longer present or alive. Give yourself permission to be forgiven—talk to yourself in a mirror if need be.

Accept that you are human and you will make mistakes for as long as you live. Learn from the lesson and strive to do better going forward.

**Ghost voices** haunt you with their whispered taunts about your shortcomings, inadequacies, failures, and "shoulds"—what you should or should not be doing.

They may come from your childhood—teachers, coaches, classmates, or playmates—persons who may barely remember you at all.

Family ghost voices can be powerful, especially if those persons are no longer living.

Sometimes the ghost voices are your own from the past, born of assumptions that were never true.

Ghost voices are figments of your continued imagination. As long as you believe in them, they exist. As soon as you deprive them of your energy, they evaporate.

Try picturing them rising like smoke toward the sun where they dissipate and disappear.

Do you remember the *Wizard of Oz* scene where Dorothy accidentally splashes the wicked witch with a bucket of water and she melts away?

Don't you have a bucket in that raft of yours? Why not drench your ghost voices and watch them melt down into nothingness, after which you can toss the pointed hat overboard and smile at how much lighter and happier your raft feels.

**Perpetrator stowaways** are the ones who did you wrong. It doesn't matter if they are actually guilty or not; what matters is that you believe them to be.

I find it crucial to remember that what they did "to me" actually had nothing to do with me at all. Their behavior is a reflection of their own junky issues. Being the recipient of their nastiness doesn't mean I caused it or deserved it.

Maybe this person was meant to help me develop new strengths or shift me towards a better direction.

I must first accept that no acknowledgement of wrongdoing is going to come. I don't have to be okay with what happened, and I don't have to forgive and forget. I can let a higher power take care of the forgiveness for now, and while it may be impossible to forget, by cutting off the energy that feeds it, the stowaway will eventually fade away.

Picture yourself fanning ongoing flames of fury and resentment over the perpetrators in your raft. Can you see the result? Is this person worth the destruction of your own raft?

Imagine stowaway conversations on the plastic tape that is used in movie reels. We replay scenes and conversations over and over again; what was said, what we should have said, should have done, and on and on. With each playing, we ramp up our angst, our pain, and our stress.

One way to stop replaying this dreaded tape is to unravel it. Let this signify the unraveling of all the hurt and anger and pain. Then just throw the whole thing away. It's a jumbled mess. It always was. It no longer has any value or any use. Good riddance. Get it out of your raft, and forget you ever held on to it.

I do know that the more you practice what I call baggage control, the better you get at it. Recognize the silver linings to be found in the situation. There is almost always something to be grateful for.

In some cases, you might just have to remind yourself that things could actually have been worse, even if you can't imagine how.

I have found it helpful to picture the baggage being handed to me, and my refusing to accept it. Or, I imagine packing the baggage tightly into packages, tossing it back into the rafts from which it came, then watching it all float away.

This is because I finally realized that much of the baggage we haul around was really someone else's negative stuff to start with.

We can consciously examine some of our baggage and learn from it so that we don't put ourselves in the position of accumulating anything like it ever again.

In my darkest moments, I kept telling myself that everything was a blessing in disguise, even if it didn't make sense yet. I repeated it constantly, going through the motions until I could begin to believe it. I'm mostly there, but it's still an ongoing process.

It's important to point out that getting rid of baggage is rarely a one-time event. Most of us throw it out, pick it back up, and throw it out again multiple times before we finally manage to let it go for good.

Don't beat yourself up if it takes years to free yourself from a lifetime of accumulated stuff. If you can lighten your load just a little each day, while avoiding the addition of new baggage, you'll make progress.

# Who is in Your Raft?

THE COURSE YOUR RAFT TAKES is affected by life conditions, certainly, but this direction is profoundly affected by how you paddle. And, if you relinquish your paddle to another person, it shouldn't come as a surprise that you often find yourself somewhere you didn't wish to be.

Who did you invite into your raft? Who have you allowed to hijack your raft? Who has hijacked your paddle? What's the difference?

First of all, it's important to understand that if someone is causing you significant distress, you have, at least temporarily, brought that person aboard.

Not every unwelcome passenger intended to get into your raft; you pull many of them in yourself! Think about this when you have an unpleasant interaction with anyone at all. The guy who ran the light and then gave you the finger? Don't drag him in; leave him in his own raft!

As you become aware of the unwanted "guests with baggage" you have been bringing into your raft, you will get better at leaving them where you found them.

The person who hijacks your paddle just wants you to do their bidding. The raft hijacker wants to control your life. One can lead to the other.

A person who has hijacked your raft has totally taken over your life. You are living your life within the context of the other person with little to no life of your own. What you do, what you like and how you think are really the other person's thoughts and preferences.

If you suddenly find yourself doing things or going places you don't like, someone has hijacked your raft and/or your paddle.

It's vital to realize that you have been complicit in the hijacking. Losing control of your raft or paddle can be a subtle and gradual process, but part of you knew something wasn't right long before you acknowledged it—the inner compass we ignore.

Remember, the idea is for us to share the river and come together in love, friendship, support, and cooperation. We aren't supposed to spend our energy trying to hijack someone else's raft or paddle, or defending ourselves from hijackers!

Let's start with the people who most commonly hijack paddles.

The people we depend on for our monthly paychecks or who hold our career in their hands wield a very specific kind of power over us, but I cannot think of a single situation in which a boss should have control of your raft. It happens, but more often, the boss just hijacks your paddle.

There are a variety of occasions in which you may find yourself playing tug of war with a boss over your paddle. For example, are you often forced to miss important family occasions because of last minute demands by your boss?

You will have to decide, on a case-by-case basis, where the balance is between choosing to do something necessary that you'd rather avoid, and feeling pressured or required to do things you find unfair or even distasteful on a regular basis.

New jobs, businesses and careers often require periods of personal sacrifice, but if the situation is far from ideal, maybe it's time for you to start lining up another position or another career.

Achieving an agreeable balance between the demands of your job and your personal life is not a trivial matter; dissatisfaction with one's job is directly related to health and wellbeing.

This is a difficult time for many businesses and it is important to clarify the expectations and requirements of all concerned in a workplace. But, is your job your life? Are you willing to compromise what really matters to you? For how long? Can you make some adjustments so your income and your essential happiness are more in balance?

Your answers will determine how you handle your situation. Be true to yourself and decide where the healthy boundary line needs to be drawn between your life and your work, and then take back your paddle.

If you work at home, the division between work and life can be especially fuzzy. Having a room dedicated only to work can help so that at the end of the work day, you can close the door and symbolically go home. A separate "home" desk may be necessary to make this work so that temptation to do a little "work" work (since you're there anyway) doesn't slip in.

What if you are your own boss?

It can still be a struggle, and your "boss" alter ego can be as demanding as a separate person. Think of this situation as you having two paddles.

Very few people are in the fortunate position of being able to use both at the same time to propel themselves smoothly in a direction that satisfies the essential self as well as the demands of a job. For most of us, it will be a juggling act requiring significant effort.

Decide when your workday paddle needs to be put down, and what steps you could take to make life better for yourself. Be clear about your expectations and the realities of your situation.

The next category of unwanted passengers is the "persona non grata." *Persona non grata* is a phrase that means "unwelcome person", so really anyone who tries to get into our rafts should be an unwelcomed person, but as we all know, some are more "non grata" than others!

When an interaction with someone results in you feeling resentful, becoming irritable, or losing sleep, beware. Personas non grata are interlopers who push their ways into our lives in ways we find intrusive and uncomfortable.

The telemarketer might just be doing his job, but we usually consider him a persona non grata.

Another example of a persona non grata is the friend or family member who exhausts you with her endless tales of woe and misery. (You know, the one who sucks every last molecule of feel good energy from your day.) If you groan when you see her number come up on the phone ID, rest assured you have a persona non grata on the line. You may love her, but at times, she brings more stress than joy with her.

Another type is the club, school, or church volunteer who browbeats or "guilts" you into working on some project. This persona non grata doesn't want your raft, she just wants to control your paddle for a while. She will smile sweetly as she rips it slowly but forcefully from your grasp.

The ex-spouse is a special kind of persona non grata. Establishing healthy boundaries will be crucial for dealing with this person.

In fact, dealing with any persona non grata really boils down to healthy boundaries. The persona non grata does not bring out the best in us. Why in the world would we let them have our paddles or get in our rafts?

Helping others is important but we should also feel comfortable putting ourselves first when we need to. There are times when we simply cannot be of help to another person, or take any more time away from our families.

You don't have to be a slave to your phone or any kind of social media. Who said you had to be available to others all the time?

All you people pleasers out there, make a list of kind but firm ways to just say no. Practice saying a few of them out loud.

"I would love to help, but it just isn't possible for me right now" or "I have other plans" are perfectly acceptable responses, and no further explanation is required.

One of my visualizations involves interaction or observation from the cozy comfort of my peaceful raft while happily acknowledging that I am not obligated to extend my paddle or boarding privileges to anyone.

## LOVED ONES: THE TIES THAT BIND.

We don't get to choose our family members, and most of us will remain bound to them in some way our entire lives. While our connections to cousins, aunts, uncles, and other more distant family members tend to be looser, we are usually fairly closely tied to parents, children, siblings, and grandparents.

In the case of our immediate family, we form attachments to one another in special ways that create almost tangible ties between rafts. It is in our nature to build a strong tie that binds us to our children.

We may create close ties to our partners, but those ties are rarely as strong as the ones we have to our children, siblings, and parents. It may be cliché, but years of sociological study have shown that early familial ties really are stronger than others we form later in life. It doesn't mean they are necessarily happier or healthier relationships, just stronger.

As adults, we sometimes have to contend with parents who continue trying to paddle our rafts.

I wasn't strong enough to keep my dad from hijacking my paddle until I was nearly 40 years old, so I literally kept an ocean between us for most of my adult life. When it became clear that I would lose my father sooner rather than later, I made the decision to return to the U. S. and actually live within walking distance of my parents' house.

He went back to his efforts to control and I quietly held my tongue and my paddle with a smile. Once he learned that I wouldn't give in, he stopped trying to take over—remarkable. We mended fences, but it was another lesson I wish I'd learned sooner.

If you are currently dealing with a parent or in-law who gets miffed when you don't do as they wish, you are probably playing tug of war over your paddle. There may not be any overt struggle going on, but if you are feeling resentful or made to feel that you "should" be doing more, it is vital that you decide what issues belong in whose raft.

Are you doing your best to do what you can? Have you been as honest and straightforward as possible about any potential issues?

After my father died, I did my best to try to get my mother involved in social or church groups of some sort. She had never been a club person, she said. She had always loved to entertain, so I encouraged her to have guests over. But she was reluctant to do so because she was convinced that no one had time for her. She loved going places, but rarely went anywhere unless I went with her. Eventually, she preferred to stay home for holidays and special occasions.

Caught between not leaving her alone and missing activities at my in-laws' homes put me in an impossible position countless times. I always felt guilty for not getting my mother out more often, and as I currently go through my own period of alone-ness, I hurt for how very lonely she must have felt.

Only years after her death am I finally coming to grips with the fact that as long as she was physically and mentally capable of making plans, her loneliness and social isolation were primarily a result of her choices. During the brief period in which she was not capable of taking care of herself, I did everything I could have done. I have to accept that I did my best most of the time, and let go of what was not my responsibility.

If we all live long enough, adult children one day take on parental roles as aging parents begin to depend on their children for increasing assistance. It is important to recognize that this kind of transition is not easy for anyone involved. Loving and honest discussion about each person's needs and boundaries will be crucial in helping everyone adjust to constantly changing roles.

Siblings may grow up with the same parents, but few of them actually grow up in the same family. Today, that can mean different parents, step-family members, and half-siblings. However, what I really mean is that even siblings from intact families have different perspectives of their family life.

My brother is ten years younger than I am. I was an only child for the first ten years of my life and have many typical first child traits. Then, I left home and he became an only child. He has many first child traits, too. We grew up in very different family environments, even though we came from the same home with the same parents.

Full, half, or step siblings have special bonds, whether they are of closeness or avoidance. Competition for parental approval or love can continue for a lifetime, as can caring, support, and cooperation. The death of the parents can totally change the relationships, but the impact depends on the ages of everyone involved and the existing dynamics of the immediate and extended families.

Spouses and partners are another issue entirely. Too many of us have a "can't live with him; can't live without him" mentality. I am convinced that much of this is a result of failing to establish healthy boundaries early on.

I was first married at a very young age because I allowed my dad to hijack my paddle. I compounded that mistake by allowing him to pass that control directly to my first husband. The marriage ended a decade later when I finally grew a brain and a backbone, took back my raft and paddle, and sent him back to his own raft. Finally establishing boundaries didn't go over well with him, but it sure was liberating for me!

Being part of a couple means sharing joys and weathering storms together. It means holding one another's hands—both literally and figuratively—to steady one another, to offer love, support, and comfort. But the balance between intimacy and healthy boundaries is vital.

You should never be expected to sacrifice the integrity of your very essence. Giving from the heart is amazing and fills one with joy and satisfaction. Receiving with the heart is humbling and healing. When no amount of giving satisfies the receiver, the giver becomes heavily burdened with resentment.

What if you are very ill? What a blessing to have someone you trust to paddle for you when you simply cannot. The key is in knowing when the paddle needs to be returned to its rightful owner. Giving and receiving, while safeguarding the integrity of the rafts and respecting healthy boundaries, are the delicate elements of the balancing act.

Healthy boundaries should surround every raft so this also implies that we shouldn't try to invade another person's raft or try to hijack their paddle.

Think about this carefully and ask yourself the following questions:

Are friends, coworkers, or loved ones becoming increasingly impatient with your "requests?" Are you constantly frustrated at what others seem reluctant to do for you? Are you regularly hurt over the inability of your loved ones to meet your needs?

Are you one of those people who doesn't take "no" for an answer? Are you the one who says, "jump", and expects everyone around you to answer, "how high?" Do you find your ability to do this amusing?

If the answer to any of the above is a yes, maybe you have a history of attempted paddle hijacking. Perhaps you're used to getting your own way, and never realized that you have, in fact, been hijacking the paddles of those around you.

Maybe you're expecting too much from other people, or it could be that your expectations are reasonable, but the other person does not have the capacity to give you what you need. If your needs are not being met, it is up to you to decide what needs to change—your expectations and needs, or how to satisfy them.

Forcing others to do what you want them to do, no matter how you do it, is a violation of healthy boundaries, and won't make for a good relationship in the long run. Would you like to be on the receiving end of someone just like you?

If you are experiencing extreme stress because your adult loved one is not doing what you believe he or she should do, then it's a sure sign that you are trying to hijack them. It doesn't matter if you are the multi-tasking paddling magician, you must not try to paddle someone else's raft!

Do you try to force a loved one to do the right thing for their own good, even after they have made it abundantly clear that they neither want your help nor intend to follow your suggestions? Do you try to save them from themselves at your own peril?

You can prod, plead, and beg your loved one to do what you think is right for them, but ultimately you cannot paddle another person's raft, nor are you responsible for the choices that your loved ones make. The consequences of their actions may impact you both, but forcing your will on them is unlikely to be a successful long-term solution.

Keep in mind that if you are trying to paddle someone else's raft, you still have to keep your own on course. Needless to say, that doesn't work well, either.

Trying to paddle someone else's raft creates a stressful situation for you as well as the other person. You are attempting to hijack their paddle, if not their raft! Trust me, they won't appreciate it.

I can picture myself a few years ago—"Honey, don't go that way. There's a waterfall over there. Please, honey. Can't you hear it? Come this way. I don't want you to go over the edge! Paddle this way, come on, help me paddle you back this way. Can't you see that you will die if you keep going that way?"

My intentions were all based on love and not wanting to lose my spouse, but I would eventually lose him anyway. Life for both of us would certainly have been less stressful if I had stopped trying to paddle his raft, even if that had meant watching him take a faster, more direct route to his final destination.

Easier said than done, of course, but I have learned the lesson; each of us is on our own personal journey.

Does it seem as if you're always in the middle of some storm? Are the storms of your creation, or are you caught up in someone else's?

If you always seem to be the one at the center of the storms, perhaps it's time to figure out why.

Do you unwittingly create storms in an effort to get someone's attention? Your own soul's perhaps? Storms are often the result of intense frustration and a lack of satisfaction with one's life.

What load are you carrying that causes so much distress you feel the need to express it in dramatic storms, some of which batter those around you?

If you aren't able to get a handle on it yourself, I encourage you to consider professional advice. A non-involved third party might be able to help you pinpoint and quell the causes of the storms you create. Some people live their entire lives in one storm after the other. There are even people who appear to think that stormy weather makes their lives exciting.

If you work, socialize, or share space with someone like this, you will eventually have to either limit the time you spend in their storm, or find ways of creating an oasis of calm that buffers you from the endless squalls of wind, rain, thunder, and lightning.

While it isn't fair for anyone to drag us into their personal storm and expect us to save them, we also have to learn to recognize and avoid the storms that aren't of our own creation.

If you were actually in the middle of an ocean in a tiny raft, you wouldn't dream of paddling straight into a hurricane that you could see coming, would you? But how many times have you virtually done exactly that in your personal life? I know I have.

It is imperative that you not allow yourself to be beaten down by someone who lashes out at whoever happens to be near. Physical and/or emotional distance may be your only way out, and this might be a five-minute escape or one that lasts a lifetime.

You may have co-workers and friends who are stormy weather people, but chances are you either rarely see that side of them, or you have already learned to keep your distance. When it's a family member, the situation can be harder to avoid or to bear.

Let's address the close family member who causes you really intense stress. I'm not referring here to the normal differences in opinion or lifestyle that involve sporadic arguments or occasional moments of tension. I'm talking about the people who create veritable tornado strength storms that often leave a trail of destruction in their path.

I call these difficult individuals "lightning bolts." At one end of the scale, they may be control-freak types that only occasionally erupt into full lightning bolts. At their most extreme, they are toxic persons.

No matter what you do, hyper-sensitive lightning bolts are often dissatisfied with anything you say or do, and for them a good defense is always a strong offense.

There's no predicting what might set them off. Sunny blue skies can darken in an instant as thunder begins rolling and lightning strikes begin.

The lightning bolt finds fault with trivialities, and reacts to imagined offenses and attacks. The lightning bolt storm can flatten you before you know what hit you.

You try to get along. You try to explain. You throw your hands up in exasperation. You cry. You walk away feeling exhausted and weary and sad and defeated. It happens over and over again.

More often than not, it boils down to give and take. One takes and takes, and the other gives and gives. You know what I mean. You give an inch, she takes a foot. You give a foot, she demands a yard. You give a yard, she wants a mile…..It never ends. It's their way or no way, and the standard they expect will always be just out of your reach.

People who regularly take more than they give are trying to fill an emptiness within themselves caused by a hurtful experience from their past. Until they figure this out, and resolve to end it, nothing will change.

It often happens that the person at the root of the emptiness is clueless or incapable of understanding what they did, or is no longer around to be confronted.

So, these lightning bolts really are victims, but it's not an excuse for their behavior. The anger and abuse directed at you is almost always misdirected.

Maybe you're the recipient of these lightning strikes because the person (ironically!) knows that you love her, so it is safe to lash out at you—her spouse, sister, mother, or daughter.

Lightning bolts feel entitled to hijack rafts and paddles right and left. They are used to getting their own way and fail to realize the harm they do. Rafts and paddles are surrendered because the thunder and lightning that would come with refusing is just not worth it.

What the lightening bolt fails to realize is that she is hurting herself. She can't see that what she is dishing out is emotional bullying. She may think of herself as a victim—no one understands her or cares about her. Sadly, lightning bolt people often push away the very people who love them most.

Here is what I tell my clients who find themselves in this type of difficult situation and ask my advice:

Choose to love the person, not their behavior. Know that hurt and fear is behind almost everything spouting from their mouth. Realize that nothing you say or do is likely to matter much, because this is rarely about you.

Establish your personal boundary line. Be mindful that it won't make much difference to the lightning bolt where the line is. Any boundary will be unacceptable, and since she may not understand her own behavior, there's no way for you to please her.

Remember, your personal boundary line is the edge of your comfort zone. It is where you decide what, or what not to tolerate. It is the limit of time, energy, money, etc. you are willingly able to give.

Clarify what you can or cannot do. Specify what is and isn't acceptable to you as best you can. Express your unconditional love simply and openly.

When the inevitable storm erupts, safeguard your personal boundary. Sending nothing but thoughts of love outward is a powerful strategy.

Don't allow yourself to be lured into creating your own storm to add to theirs. Don't argue, don't fight—you cannot win. Say as little as possible. Few tirades continue when there is no response. Retreat when the time is right. It's almost always possible to paddle away to calmer water; it just isn't always easy to do so.

If you manage not to generate your own wind and lightning, and you can find relative peace in your raft, that may be the best you can hope for. It's not up to you to calm another's storm, but you might be able to diffuse it. It will take practice plus trial and error to learn what works best for you in your situation.

If you've been living your life trying to make yourself as small as possible to avoid being a target, to avoid confrontation, or to avoid upsetting the other person, paddling away may be long overdue.

Unfortunately, some of you may be dealing with truly toxic loved ones—these are the persons whose personal storms are typhoons. Lightning bolts may be upsettingly noisy or dramatic, but the toxic person has the potential to sink a ship.

The toxic person is self-destructive and may be waging war on those closest to him or her in the process. Drug and/or alcohol abuse may be involved, or there may be behavioral addictions such as gambling or promiscuous infidelity.

Physical violence and/or emotional abuse is occurring or escalating. Your own physical, mental, and/or emotional well-being is being affected.

Trust has been destroyed, but the person attempts to guilt you into trusting them one more time when they need something from you.

If the situation is causing problems with other close relationships, or you have begun to worry or even fear for your own or other loved ones' safety, it's time to comprehend that something needs to change sooner rather than later.

If you are remaining in a toxic partner's storm because you fear reprisal or "being alone," realize that you are probably currently paddling and bailing furiously merely to stay afloat.

Seek outside help! Don't fool yourself into thinking this situation will just go away on its own or resolve itself. Professional guidance can help you in countless ways. There are support groups out there for adults and children dealing with toxic family members.

If the situation is the result of substance abuse, addiction, or mental illness, and the person receives the help he or she needs, it may possible to re-establish the relationship in the future.

It may be necessary to distance yourself from this family member for an extended time in order to protect yourself or other loved ones. Safe shelters for women and their children quietly exist in most communities and can receive you at any time, day or night. Many churches offer non-denominational counseling even to those who can't afford to pay for it, and they may also be able to help find a safe place for you to stay.

Quite often, friends and extended family members have already offered their help—accept it! Don't be ashamed to reach out.

Toxic family members can create situations that are far beyond the scope of this book. If you are caught in one of these, please take my advice and seek professional help and support.

## FAMILIES WITH INFANTS AND CHILDREN

A pregnant woman has her infant within her raft with her, of course. After a baby is born, its little raft depends on someone else's raft for its very survival.

So imagine the baby's raft now within a parent's raft. It may move between rafts, but for at least a few months it will always need to be safe in another's. Picturing this can help some people understand that their raft, their lives, are no longer totally their own. Babies are totally dependent upon someone else for all their care, and a baby's raft adds considerable responsibility to the person whose raft it resides in.

Infants have little choice but to go along with whomever they are attached to. They will share whatever the parent experiences, including joy, calm, and happiness, or stress, anger, depression, and anxiety. Once they can move around, their raft gradually moves outside their caretaker's raft.

The younger the child, the shorter the tie will be. A six-month-old infant's raft may be lashed tightly to its parent's raft. As the child becomes more independent, the ties begin to lengthen. A three year old, as we all know, works hard to stretch those ties, as does the thirteen and eighteen year old!

Let's assume for a moment that a child's raft is held between two parents' rafts. Picture these three rafts moving down the stream. It's a fairly stable configuration.

Sometimes it will be necessary for one parent to pull the child closer while the other provides more slack. If both parents work together well, the child's journey down this section of the stream can be fairly smooth. The inevitable storms, rapids, and obstacles can be dealt with and learned from.

Now picture two parents managing several children's rafts. Not so easy now. There will be a lot of trial and error. Each addition will require more communication, flexibility, and willingness to learn new techniques. Recognizing and balancing priorities and individual needs becomes much more important and harder to achieve. Cooperation, understanding, respect, and patience will be crucial.

Now throw in the fact that we are all human, we all make lots of mistakes, and we all want our needs met. Imagine all the ropes and rafts. Imagine what happens as they all move downstream together as the parents try to keep everything under control. No wonder families experience varying degrees of chaos! The term "dysfunctional" applies to all of us at some point.

Up until a few generations ago, there were extended family and close community support systems for all of us. Grandparents, aunts, uncles, and siblings often stepped forward to become caretakers, guides, and sources of strength and wisdom. They helped provide safe harbors during stormy times. Can you picture this larger network of connected rafts? Can you imagine the support and stability that this created?

With smaller families and the scattering of family members across long distances, this kind of support is harder to find. Interestingly, grandparents are once again being called on to help with child rearing. Unfortunately, they are trying to do so with fewer resources for their own needs than ever before.

Unless they are infants, your children belong in their own rafts. You keep their raft safely attached to yours, but you each have slightly different perspectives as you experience the journey down stream. However, what has happened if you turn around and find children in your raft?

Remember, you have either given them permission to come on board or you have invited them in. What's wrong with that, you may ask.

Well, there are many reasons why we need to let children retain their own rafts. The primary one is that the boundaries become blurred for parent and child. The parent eventually loses control of her hijacked raft and the child misses the initial opportunity to develop some important skills. When a parent is always immediately present to fulfill every need, there is no need to learn to wait or to consider that someone else's needs might be important. There is no need to develop impulse control or to exercise the imagination.

Now, what about the parent whose child is in her raft? When mom can't get enough sleep because the six year old likes to stay up until 10 pm, something is wrong.

Parents can certainly decide when and how often a child's opinions and preferences can be honored and acted upon, but I am seeing far too many instances in which mom and dad are frazzled and overwhelmed because the children have near total control of all the rafts and paddles. Most parents wouldn't dream of letting their child control their paddles on a real white water river, yet this is what they are doing with their very lives.

Parents do need to have some private time without their kids. It isn't always easy to find qualified, trustworthy child care for little ones, but it can be done. Mom should be able to get away for an evening with her friends without having to justify it to her children.

The bottom line is that children should not be paddling their parents' rafts and as the children grow, parents need to gradually allow their children to do more of their own paddling. Eventually it will be time for almost every child to be launched into his or her own life. I do believe our children face more stress in their every day lives than ever before. It's a complicated and changing world they will be facing, and they need our guidance to be prepared. I'd like to share two stories with you about helping children learn to paddle their own rafts.

Every parent is familiar with the "I forgot my _____" phone call. This usually means mom making a sudden run to the school to deliver the homework, project, lunch, permission slip, or money that failed to make it to school that day.

Beginning in middle school, I agreed to do this only one time per semester, unless I was already going to the school for another reason. Otherwise, the consequences were theirs to deal with. They didn't call often, preferring to come up with alternative solutions to their problem when possible, to save their call for a more urgent occasion. They never used up their calls.

A friend once explained to me why, despite our same ages, he was behind me in high school.

It turns out his sloppy school performance in middle school left him a mere half a point short of what was required to be promoted to high school. It wasn't that he couldn't do better; he just let things slide.

He pleaded with two teachers to bump up his grades, to no avail. He could have made the grades up in summer school, but his parents would not rearrange their lives to provide his transportation to the school thirty minutes away. He was left with no option but to repeat the grade while his friends moved on to high school without him.

Can you imagine a parent doing that today? It was a hard lesson, but experiencing the consequences of his actions was a valuable gift. Do you think his parents lost sleep over their decision? I doubt it. The problem and solution belonged in his raft, not theirs, so they had no reason to be stressed by it. I suspect "live and learn" was how they were raised, and they applied it to their son.

This hardworking man has been a successful business owner all his life, and is one of the most dependable individuals I know.

He probably would have done well anyway, but the episode definitely shaped his behavior in a positive way. He said it certainly motivated him to do better in school from then on!

As our children grow and mature, the ties that connect them to us lengthen and allow them to become more independent, make their own mistakes, and discover their own path. The tie stretches so thin sometimes we fear it will break, but it nearly always holds so that our children can find their way back to us throughout our lives. I try to imagine the ties beginning to dissolve when children are ready to move ahead on their own; to free them to begin their own individual journeys as young adults, to chart their own courses, and make their own choices. Just because we are no longer attached to our children's rafts doesn't mean that all parental ties dissolve, of course. Primal love creates powerful connections that are unaffected by time or distance. It may be complicated and filled with joy or angst, but the tie is forever there. Just as we are always our parents' children in some ways, we are also forever our children's parents.

# The Storm of Divorce

Divorce eventually touches most of us in some way. I have a section of its impact on families with children following this one, but you may find both worthwhile.

Few transitions cause as much emotional turmoil as divorce, whether you are the one who filed for it or are the one on the receiving end. Unless you've experienced it for yourself, it's difficult to fathom the complex depths of pain a divorce can cause.

I've seen clients, friends, and loved ones of all ages brought to their knees in anguish as they ended what they thought would be "forever." There's nothing flippant about divorce. I don't know of anyone who has ever skipped down the street to the divorce lawyer as if this was an "oops, changed my mind" decision.

I'm going to briefly share my experiences with divorce because I want you to understand that I do know how hard this particular journey can be.

I've been through divorce three times, and the very act of revealing this to you still ties my stomach in knots. Society will generally give you a pass on one divorce, but two or more mean you deal with a lot of raised eyebrows and judgment.

Twice, after years of turmoil, I was forced to end impossible situations. Both spouses made the process as difficult as possible, and with a young child involved in each, it was exhausting.

The third divorce was thrust on me when I could least handle it, and knowing that my husband was not entirely capable of making this decision, tore me apart. His death a few months later took me to a place that was very hard to climb out of.

In 2014, I chose to have my maiden name restored. It was a highly emotional decision that I spent months deliberating over, but once it was done I felt that I had finally released the last anchor holding me back.

Each of us must do what is right for us and letting go of reminders of pain, betrayal, or any type of baggage is a necessary part of moving forward with a renewed sense of purpose. Sometimes this means redecorating your room, and sometimes it means changing your name. Whatever uplifts your heart and soul to a more healing place is worth doing.

Give yourself time to mourn the death of your marriage, with all its memories and dreams. The loss of an entire family you were once a part of can be a very sad part of readjusting to life after divorce.

Love may have been lost, or simply may not have been enough to sustain the marriage. There's nothing wrong with continuing to love your ex-spouse. Accept that mixed emotions are part of all breakups.

It's normal to be upset or angry for a while, but don't let your storm go on for too long. Make sure you don't become the raft with its own dark cloud constantly hovering overhead. This will not serve you well.

Recognize any gifts the marriage brought you. Find your own reasons to be grateful for the good "unintended" consequences of your marriage and of the divorce.

Take time to learn more about yourself now that you are single again. Go at your own pace with the understanding that if something isn't a good fit for you, you aren't obligated to continue. Be willing to try new things. Join groups you might like. Take a trip. Don't be afraid to venture out alone. Becoming comfortable with your own company is a very good thing.

You will survive and be happy again. Make a conscious effort to learn from these hard lessons. This opportunity to renew yourself and your life will lead you to wonderful people and places you might have missed otherwise.

Most of my discussion on baggage is applicable to divorce; certainly the sections on stowaways will resonate and be helpful to many of you. I encourage you to reread those sections as you go through the various stages of your healing process.

One of the positive consequences of divorce is that you are given the chance to make meaningful changes going forward. As you release baggage relating to the relationship that is ending, you also have a golden opportunity for ridding yourself of baggage that may have contributed to the creation of a bad situation.

Please don't think that the years you invested in the marriage were wasted ones. Look for the silver linings.

I have two beautiful daughters and have had several interesting careers as a result of my marriages, and I wouldn't have missed these for the world. I was pushed to become stronger and more self-sufficient.

I hear the most anger and bitterness over financial losses, and it can be a major issue for a long time. Please re-frame your attitude as soon as you can.

I've chosen to feel that whatever I gave in love and for love was not a waste as far as my own soul goes.

That another person took advantage of my generosity is a sad reflection of their character, and I believe that sooner or later, they will have to answer for it, but that isn't in my raft. Let it go. Move forward with the satisfaction that you gave the best of yourself.

Never feel that your age limits your future after divorce. I remember being 29 and feeling I was "too old" to start all over again. Now, decades later, I find my naiveté quite amusing.

Of course, the younger you are when you go through it, the more time you might have to recover and start again, but there are no guarantees to anything in life. Being older, more mellow, and infinitely wiser can help you make much better choices for your future.

You will be forever changed by your divorce, and if you prioritize your raft by staying true to yourself, you will find reasons for gratitude.

A degree of sadness may always remain, but that's true of many difficult events in life. Just don't let it weigh you down.

If you find yourself still struggling many months after your divorce, please don't hesitate to seek professional support. I've done so many times, and just speaking to a non-involved third party can go a long way toward healing and recovery.

Regardless of your situation, when you are ready to leave the fear and pain behind, know that every single day offers you unknown opportunities for a full life of love and joy. Begin again.

## CHILDREN AND DIVORCE

Let's return to our children's rafts, now. Can you imagine what happens to a child's raft when the parents begin engage in battle or in a tug of war with their children's rafts—their very lives?

The child is caught in the middle, or left defenseless on the fringes, and in either case it is a very scary place to be.

First, the tension and discord that precedes the figurative battle creates palpable tension for everyone. It's usually clear to everyone that storm clouds are gathering. As the wind picks up, the water gets choppy. No one feels at ease. Everyone becomes more sensitive and emotional.

Some may exhibit anxiety symptoms like nightmares or acting out at school. Some try to escape and make a run for a safe harbor. Still others will hunker down or withdraw, to weather the storm as best they can. They may not know what to do, but anything seems better than doing nothing.

Yelling, fighting and physical violence are like severe thunder and lightning strikes, and the situation quickly becomes terrifying.

Sometimes the crisis passes, but many times it just becomes one in a series of storms that batters everyone caught up in it for months or years on end. Divorce or reconciliation may end the turmoil, although neither guarantees the end of stormy weather.

Everyone's situation is unique and there are no simple solutions for anyone. I offer very few suggestions here; my aim is mainly to help you visualize the situation in a different way.

The physical effect of jerking a small raft around in raging waters is representative of the emotional effect on a child of arguing, fighting, threatening, and jostling for control. They are helpless. They can't stop the storm and they can't get off the river.

Sometimes it is a relief when one parent simply lets go completely, although there are significant long-term consequences to this too, of course. The ties are still attached to the child's raft, but there is no one on the other end.

It doesn't have to be this way, even if divorce ends the marriage. I do know of people who managed to continue being good parents, even when physical distance made it more difficult.

In today's technological world, I can't imagine any adult having an excuse for losing touch with their child. Where there's a will, there is a way.

The abandoned child may come to the conclusion that no one can be trusted to be there for long, or worse, that they are not lovable enough. It's no surprise that establishing close relationships as adults becomes emotionally complicated and difficult.

Children develop their own coping mechanisms, and these may become fairly permanent characteristics as time goes by. They acquire scars and skills.

Many will be become more resilient and will learn to paddle around any obstacle and escape any whirlpool. Some will try to hide in someone else's raft, not wanting to even attempt to paddle anywhere that could potentially be dangerous. Still others will fortify their rafts and use their paddles to fend off anyone who tries to come too close.

Whatever the effect, it is likely to last a lifetime, unless they make the effort to change the response. You may realize that some of your adult behavior is a direct result of your own childhood experiences.

The vast majority of single parent families are headed by women, but there is a growing trend of mothers leaving their families, so greater numbers of fathers are suddenly finding themselves navigating unfamiliar territory as single or primary parents.

Either way, we have a parent with at least one child to escort down the river. Can you picture the juggling act when there are two or more children's rafts attached to one parent's raft?

It's hard enough when everything is calm, but if any one needs special attention, a storm comes up, or some calamity occurs, it can challenge the most adept parent.

Unfortunately, I am well acquainted with the challenges of raising children as a single parent, having done it more than once.

Altogether, I was married for 30 years, yet I was always a single mother. The fathers managed never to be very involved before or after our divorces. I certainly didn't plan my life this way, but it happened.

I did my best to minimize the effects of divorce on my daughters, but I couldn't protect them from it all. I tried to provide them with the most stable home environment possible on my end.

Sometimes I succeeded brilliantly and sometimes I failed miserably.

They each experienced the ups and downs of my life in very different ways. I fervently wish I could erase the emotional scars they carry, but I am proud of the women they've become and the lives they are building as young adults.

I grew up in an "intact" family, but I acquired plenty of scars and skills, as well. Intact families are not always healthier than divorced ones. My own family situation was complicated, as almost all are. Much is hidden behind closed doors. Adulthood and hindsight reveal what is not always apparent when we are children.

Would I have been better off if my parents had divorced? In my case, I doubt it, but I'll never know.

My point is this: I believe that some relationships can be salvaged and many cannot. Children are vulnerable but resilient. The same is true for adults. Establishing healthy boundaries that are as fair and respectful as possible for everyone involved is the best scenario.

Grandparents can be godsends but may need guidance to support your efforts at minimizing the harm. Your children will benefit from every relationship that gives them loving attention. Encourage closeness if possible.

I don't believe anyone should stay in a situation that involves highly stressful battles on a regular basis, be they emotional, verbal, or physical ones.

Imagine yourself in a raft in the middle of a storm that tosses you from one side to the other; that calms for a short time only to come out of nowhere and slam you again and again, with no end in sight. This is no way for anyone to live.

Every adult and every child deserves a chance to live without distress, without chaos, and without fear. Sometimes, divorce is the only way to achieve this.

No matter your age, if you are a child of divorce, I sincerely hope this helps put things into perspective for you and allows you to move forward with a lighter heart and a little less baggage.

If a parent abandoned you after a divorce, I want to emphasize that their behavior was never about you, but is a sad reflection of the parent, and his or her issues and inability to be a parent. Be sure to read the sections about baggage for help in dealing with this devastating, but increasingly common, situation.

Regardless of the circumstances surrounding your separation or divorce—whether it happened decades ago or last week, or is happening now, or looming in the near future—please consider professional support for yourself and your family at any point in time.

I have an amazing support group of friends, but I've sought professional guidance many times over the years when my personal situations reached critical or overwhelming levels. Please don't let pride, shame, or cost prevent you from reaching out for help. Affordable options are available in every area. It's no one's business but yours and it could make a world of difference for you.

Divorce is surely one of the most heart-wrenching experiences we ever go through, especially when children are involved, but sometimes it is the best thing you can do for yourself and for your children.

Once you have come through the storm, you will marvel at the relative calm and wonder how you ever withstood so much bad weather. There will still be difficult days ahead, but you are stronger and more capable than ever. It will be better.

# Your Raft, Your Journey

I hope that over the next few days, you will continue to visualize your raft and your journey. Now that you have a different perspective of the raft scenario, I encourage you to reread the Natural Rules. I want you to enjoy a journey that fills your raft with love and purpose, satisfaction and happiness.

The most common regret voiced by people at the end of their lives is that they wished they had risked more and been truer to themselves in living their lives. Let us not reach the end of our journey regretting a life unlived to its fullest potential—unspoken love, wasted time and worry over needless things, or precious moments that went unrecognized as the gifts they were.

Memories are double-edged swords. Revisiting the past to bring joyful gifts back into your present is a wonderful thing. Wishing one could go back to undo some of it is a tremendous waste of energy and life. Focusing on the past is the equivalent of dragging an anchor while trying to paddle forward.

Learn your lessons and adjust your present course accordingly. The process begins in your heart, soul, and attitude, and leads to your actions. The present is the only place where creating change is possible and where your choices truly make a difference.

Do your best each day and then let tomorrow come. You can't change the future by stressing over it today, but you sure can make your life more miserable.

If there's a problem, can you identify whose it is? Who exactly does it cause problems for? Does it belong in your raft? Is it part of your journey?

Your raft is separate from every other raft. It's always a wonderful thing to help one another, but there are times we must say, "not my raft, not my journey."

Be careful that what feels like a problem to you isn't actually your discomfort with someone else's choices or paths. They are not your responsibility. Maybe the problem is nonexistent except for your perception of it. In that case, it shouldn't be part of your journey. If you realize there is a problem but it doesn't belong in your raft, you might say, "not my raft, not my problem."

I want you to lighten your load, and become more particular about what you choose to carry with you. Start wherever feels best. Sometimes unloading a major stowaway results in associated baggage going with it. Other times, you need to start with smaller things and work your way up.

Consider your own behavior, as well, and make an effort not to pass your own problems to another person. If you realize you've already been loading a loved one's raft down with your baggage, let them know you want it back so you can dump it yourself. If you feel stuck, maybe it's time to clean out your raft. After all, it's carrying a very special soul on a very important journey.

A change of scenery can help you realize that you can alter the course of your life's journey. Take that trip you've been putting off, even if it's just an hour away.

Establish your own soothing rituals. Taking a few minutes to sip a cup of calming tea can give you a chance to unwind. Listening to music while relaxing in the tub can quiet your mind. Regular routines can keep you sane when everything else is falling apart.

Make a conscious effort to stop multitasking! You won't really get more done; you will only make yourself feel rushed and scattered. Completing one task at a time really is more efficient and calming.

Slow down and create your life a moment at a time. Do whatever you're doing with more care and less mental urgency to get to the next thing.

When I stopped working and multitasking during my lunch break and took time just to enjoy my food while watching birds or the butterflies in my garden, it was amazing how much more productive I was afterwards. No books, no phone, no computer. Try it!

Create little islands of calm in your life. Treat yourself to a massage. Go for a short walk. Meet a friend for a quick cup of coffee in the middle of a crazy day, or take a catnap before a busy late afternoon. You may think you have no time for things like this, but trust me, you will be in a better mood and have more energy later by taking a break when you most need it. A day spent in pajamas doing "nothing" may be just what you need! You aren't a machine. You're a human being that needs time to breathe and smile and relax. You are worth being pampered and nurtured.

Always give yourself permission to cry or laugh, to be busy or to be quiet. Allow yourself space and time to ponder and daydream and wonder. No holding back! Don't be afraid of your own thoughts and dreams—let them flow freely and see what comes to you.

Make meals special, especially if you are living alone. No eating standing at the counter or eating straight out of the container. Serve yourself like you were royalty. I recently found a beautiful capiz shell tray to carry my meal to wherever I plan to eat since I often eat on my sun porch or outside. A nice cloth napkin with my grandmother's silver napkin ring goes with it. I have a wonderful bowl that a client gifted me, and it helps remind me that I am worth taking care of. These small touches make even a simple meal feel special.

I strongly recommend making over your bedroom to make it a peaceful sanctuary to retire to when the day ends. Really. This is more important than you might imagine. Nighttime is when your body does its repair and maintenance work. It is also the place to leave the day's stresses behind so that your mind can rest.

The first five minutes of the morning set the tone for your day. What do you first see when you open your eyes? Piles of stuff can make you feel behind before the day has even begun. There should be nothing in this space that causes you stress or dismay.

This needn't require spending money. Sometimes, just making the bed each morning can be a step toward a more peaceful bedroom. See what you can remove from the space—dirty laundry, stacks of things to do, etc. Relegate these things to another room and keep clutter out of this space. Everything your eye falls on should make you feel good.

I place a high priority on comfortable bedding. One of my splurges is a silk pillowcase. Silk is gentle to skin and hair and offers a touch of luxury at the end of the day. A fresh pillow or new sheets may help. Your bed should be comfortable and conducive to a good night's sleep. A spritz of lavender is nice, too.

Before you get up each morning, tell yourself that it will be a good day, and that you will do at least one thing for yourself this day. Make it happen.

Dreading the coming day on a regular basis means it's time to make some serious changes. You don't have to leap from the bed with glee, but it should be with some degree of positive anticipation. A few minutes of evening preparation to make the next morning easier is more than worth your time.

The last minutes before you go to sleep, express gratitude for what you have and congratulate yourself for what you are doing to create a better life for yourself. Every little baby step counts!

You alone are responsible for creating your own happiness. Make time for more of the things you love. Seek the company of those who make you feel wonderful, who uplift your spirit and support your efforts. Be aware of the quality of the days that make up your life and make each one worthwhile.

In these pages I have revealed some of my most vulnerable moments to you. Every woman is stronger than she believes herself to be, but it's impossible to realize your true strength unless it's put to the test. I know you can paddle through storms and come out into the sunshine on the other side.

I want you to prioritize your raft. By that I mean that I want you to love yourself, be true to yourself, and be willing to take care of yourself. I want you to take full responsibility for your own paddle, raft, and journey. Start treating yourself as you would a very special loved one. Be kind and patient with yourself.

Explore your options. Feed the dream that keeps calling to you. Take a few steps in any direction and see where you are led. Find the voice of your higher, truer self and let her out! Walk like her, talk like her, act like her, live like her, love and nourish her soul.

We are here to paddle our own rafts, and we each have to find our own way of making the journey. Some of us will travel "merrily and gently down the stream," while others will whip through rapids anxiously seeking the next thrill, and still others will be thankful just to make it through each day. Some of us won't come to our senses until we have gone over several increasingly challenging waterfalls, but there is hope for the most hardheaded of us.

We always have choices available to us, if we are just brave enough to change course. You might find the Raft Map exercise at the end of this book helpful.

I want you to believe that life is meant to be good so that you live each day expecting the best outcomes in everything you do. I want you to find unexpected joy at every turn because you are watching for it.

It brings me great pleasure to have completed this little book and released it into the river of life that we all share. My greatest hope is that it find its way to those of you who most need what it has to offer, at the very moment it best serves you.

Whatever your journey, may it always be true!

## Implementing the concept: The Raft Map

I have designed a wonderful workshop based on Paddling Your Own Raft, and offer it to small groups several times a year. The workshop involves creating small personal rafts and using colored stones, small objects, and a crystal river to explore the concepts of the book. You can contact me for more information on how to attend this workshop or offer it to your group.

However, I wanted readers to also have a way of clarifying their personal situations above and beyond visualization. The Raft Map exercise is certainly not as striking as the workshop, but I hope many of you find it helpful.

You will need a few pieces of blank unlined letter size paper, a pen, and a pencil with an eraser.

1. Using the pen, draw an oval in the middle of the paper. This is your raft. Draw a little stick figure in it to represent yourself.
2. Now, quickly draw in the rafts (any size) of the most significant people in your life (living or deceased). Put them anywhere around you. Try not to overthink this—try to be childlike and just put them where it first occurs to you. Put names on the rafts.
3. With your pencil draw scribbly lines to show any storms you are currently aware of. Turn it over and set this sheet aside.

4. Take a fresh sheet of paper, and using a pen, list every person and piece of "baggage" that you know you are carrying—stowaways, ghost voices, personas non gratas, etc.

   Don't take more than 5-10 minutes on this. This is just a short lesson and you can do deeper work later. I just want you to identify what is uppermost in your mind at this moment—the people and stuff you are very aware of.

5. Return to your first sheet, and using a pencil, draw the following in your raft: a stick figure to represent every person from your list and a circle-like image to represent every item on your list. These can be any shape or size. Just keep piling them up in your raft.

6. OK, now it's time to take a look at what you have created.

7. Find yourself in the raft. Where are you? Sitting on top of the pile, or buried beneath it? Where is your paddle? Are you still holding it? Are there storms going on? Where do the storms tend to be? Are you in one looking out, or are you outside looking in? Which parcels in your raft are darkest or largest and heavier?

8. Who needs to be sent back to their own rafts? Connect the people in your raft to their own rafts by drawing a line between them. Imagine yourself showing them the way back to their rafts.

9. If any of the people in your raft are no longer living, why are they still in your raft? If their presence is a heavy load, you most certainly need to choose to remove them from your raft. Their journey on this particular river is over, but they will ride along with you if you let them.

    If the deceased person is there because you cherish them and their presence comforts you, consider picturing them in particularly beautiful, ephemeral rafts that glide beside you–always connected to you by love, but always in separate rafts, because as a separate soul you still have a separate journey on this river to experience. You might even imagine them traveling ahead from time to time, protecting you, guiding you, supporting you.

    If Einstein is correct, time is only an earthly human concept, and multiple time period layers of "existence" not only exist, but potentially overlap and mingle from time to time. Who's to say that our loved ones' journeys aren't continuing on another "river" or plane of existence that we know nothing of. All the more reason for each of us to occupy and paddle our own rafts.
10. I suspect your raft is very crowded. Who or what would you like to erase? Can you erase anyone you sent back to their own raft? Is there anything in your raft you can erase right this minute? Do it! How does it feel?

Fear of being alone might lead you to keep people and baggage in your raft because you aren't sure how you'll feel without them to keep you company. Don't be afraid to find out. You'll adjust!

11. Take a fresh piece of paper and draw a new raft with yourself in it. Put a smile on your face.
12. On the back, make a list of what you want to have in your raft. This requires a little more thought now, doesn't it? Your list may be really short or really long.

Did you list beautiful and positive feelings, experiences, and dreams–love, hope, strength, knowledge, travel, joy, discovery, wonder, learning, and so forth?

Remember that these take up no space or weight. You can never overload your raft with these. They create only lovely stability.

13. Draw symbols for them in your new raft. What did you end up with?

Dreams and hopes are kissing cousins, and they inspire us to seek wonderful things.

You may wish to create a more elaborate drawing later. You might keep these original drawings to remind you of what is going on and how you might resolve it. I encourage you to take at least one small step each day.

Don't expect perfect clarity. Our lives and our essential selves are always caught up in a cycle of transition and transformation.

Keep the lessons learned and let go of anything negative and harmful. Embrace the good stuff. Go forward wiser and stronger, and without fear.

# Acknowledgements

I wish to thank my deeply loved daughters and brother for their encouragement in all my endeavors. You are everything to me, and it is because of you that I have come this far with my heart and spirit intact.

My heart-felt thanks also go out to David, who has been more of a son and less of a son-in-law to me. To my uncle Jerry, cousins and other distant relatives for strengthening my Hawkins-Wyatt roots. To Dahalma for her loving support, and posthumous loving thanks to Mayra.

The truth is that I have several families—a few by blood and many by choice. It's one thing to have wonderful groups of friends when the going is good, but to have them stick with you when your life is falling apart and you're no fun to be around is a true honor. And now, you are all cheering me on as I go down this new road. I am blessed and ever so thankful to have you in my life!

To my countless friends who have been there for me in a thousand thoughtful ways—you are too many to mention all by name, but please know how grateful I am for your unwavering support—my International Lunch Club friends, high school friends, and my closest friends, especially Alison, Anne, Arlette, Glenda, Patty Jo and Susi. Special abrazos to my many life-long and dear friends in Costa Rica, and to far away Macarena and Alejandra, who prove that time and distance are nothing between true friends. To my many clients, who rallied around me to help with caring understanding, especially to Maggie who fostered and then adopted my mother's new puppy. To the special people who gave of their time and labor to help me, especially Ty, Pam, and Calvin, who went above and beyond. To the many "angels" who helped with my mother, my sincerest thanks. Most especially to Mary, who was destined to guide my mother, me, and my daughter through that long night—I am deeply and forever grateful.

Special thanks to Shellie Mitchell, the talented artist whose beautiful artwork graces the cover of this book. Our paths were meant to cross and I know that stars are shining for us.

My gratitude to the body work specialists under whose hands I have received much needed moments of relaxation and stress relief, especially Jamie Hyatt and her YL oils, Amber Vachon (AMMA), and the staff of Agota Springs.

Un millón de gracias y un fuerte abrazo to Tanya Raine, for helping me learn to laugh again through the incredible gift of her energy based healing touch.

My thanks to Don Hans & Doña Judy van der Wielen, and the entire staff of the Hotel Bougainvillea in Costa Rica, my home away from home, who always treat me so well that other guests think I'm a hotel VIP, but who went above and beyond to comfort me with hugs, treats, and special kindness during my two stays when I was grieving. You all make me feel taken care of and cared for, and have made me feel like part of your hotel family.

Special appreciation to the entire restaurant staff that caters to my every whim, and to the housekeeping staff that spoils me with flowers and attention. Special cariños to: Maritza, Leticia, and Jackie for their warm-hearted graciousness, Diego for years of kind attention to me and my family (may your new life be wonderful!), Carlos for always making me smile, Ivan for perfect cappuccinos, and Anthony for being himself. A special posthumous acknowledgement to Enrique for his old-school attention and his fun-loving humor.

Special thanks and recognition to two other places in Costa Rica where nature and good energy brought me peace and healing when I most needed it.

Finca Luna Nueva Lodge: Steven Farrell and staff, especially Ismael Torres.

Ama Tierra Yoga Retreat & Wellness Center: Bob & Jill Ruttenberg and staff, especially for their part in putting Tanya in my path.

# About the Author

Marie Elena Hawkins is a certified Holistic Nutritionist and writer. She attributes her lifelong interest in holistic living to her maternal Costa Rican grandmother who passed away in 2007 at the age of 105.

Her personal experience, bi-cultural heritage, and background as a whole foods chef and as an educator have contributed to a diverse base of knowledge and skills that help her guide women toward better health and wellbeing. While her home base is in Tennessee, she also considers Costa Rica to be her home. She has published many articles but *Paddle Your Own Raft* is her first book. She is already working on a second Paddle Your Own Raft book, as well as a memoir of her childhood experiences in Costa Rica.

**www.healthiersolutionsbymarie.com**

# About the Artist

Shellie Mitchell has a degree in Fine Arts from Appalachian State University, and says it never occurred to her to do anything other than create beautiful art.

Her inspiration comes from song lyrics, the sea, the mountains, and the colors and patterns found in nature. She captures her concepts by layering fabric over wood in a collage-like style, resulting in creations that both captivate and delight the viewer. Never still, she is a busy wife and stay at home mom who enjoys having fun with her family and friends. She currently makes her home in South Carolina. *She Never Looked Back* is one of her most popular designs. **www.shellieartist.etsy.com**

www.ingramcontent.com/pod-product-compliance
Lightning Source LLC
Chambersburg PA
CBHW031452040426
42444CB00007B/1065